VanCleave, Janice
Janice VanCleave's
play and find out
$30.00   about science

3/61
$30

Janice VanCleave's

Play and Find Out

about

Science

Easy Experiments for Young Children

John Wiley & Sons, Inc.

New York • Chichester • Brisbane • Toronto • Singapore

Copyright © 1996 by Janice VanCleave
Illustrations copyright © 1996 by Stan Tusan
Design and Production by Navta Associates, Inc.

Published by John Wiley & Sons, Inc.
All rights reserved. Published simultaneously in Canada.

Library of Congress Cataloging-in-Publication Data

VanCleave, Janice Pratt.
    [Play and find out about science}
    Janice VanCleave's play and find out about science : easy experiments for young
children / illustrated by Stan Tusan.
        p.   cm.   —(Play and find out series)
        Includes index.
        ISBN 0-471-12942-9 (cloth : alk. paper).—ISBN 0-471-12941-0 (paper : alk. paper)
        1. Physics—Experiments. 2. Chemistry—Experiments. I. Tusan, Stan. II. Title.
III. Series: VanCleave, Janice Pratt. Play and find out series.
QC25.V23   1996
530'.078—dc20   95-42938

Printed in the United States of America
10 9 8 7 6 5 4 3 2

Dedication

This book is dedicated to a special teacher whom I can proudly call my friend. She is a vivacious, energetic lady and one of the most dedicated teachers I know. Who but Laura Fields Roberts would be at Kinko's at midnight preparing papers for the next school day at St. Matthews Elementary and FedExing me comments about my experiments? May the Lord bless me with more friends like Laura.

Acknowledgments

I wish to express my appreciation to the following teachers and students, who assisted me in testing the experiments in this book:

The Lott Elementary Pre-School Inclusion Program (Lott, Texas), directed by Lisa Hall, Laurie Hoelscher, Melissa Hubby, and Judy Koenig. Another test group at the Lott Elementary School includes the following first graders who, under Ms. Hubby's guidance, helped with the testing: Matt A., Cory E., Tim H., Brian M., Alex P., Matt P., Lance S., Shannon T., and Jasmin W.

Maupin Elementary School students (Louisville, Kentucky), under the direction of Laura Roberts and her coworkers, Jackie Frost and Dawn Tarquinio: Chantelle Bartee, Eddric Beasley, Simona Bullitt, Tameika Burris, Courtney Dale, Jarrett Dennis, Adam Dodd, Heidi Dodd, Evan Doss, Erica Entrican, Candice Goodrich, Matthew Heye, Jerome Ivory, Essence Johnson, Julia Latchaw, Hunter Matson, Tierionna Morris, Hien Nguyen, Thao Nguyen, Beth Pendley, Matthew Phillips, Anita Smith, Brandon Smith, Frederick Smith, Minh Ta, Kevin Taylor, and LeAndrae Thompson.

West Point Elementary School students (West Point, California), under the direction of Karen Dickerson, Linda Gonzales, and Linda Toren: Jenell Bates, Talesha Bates, Mikaela Bianchi, Chari Coey, Jon Coey, Theresa Emond, Tasha Franz, Matthew Hoffman, Jared Link, Ashley Maynard, Kyle Owen, and William Paar.

A special note of thanks to Laura Roberts, Melissa Hubby, and Linda Toren, who took time from their busy schedules to write reviews for each experiment tested. Their comments were appreciated and invaluable.

Contents

A Letter from Janice VanCleave

Dear Friends,

Welcome to science playtime!

The scientific play activities in this book are about chemistry and physics. Very young children may not know the words "chemistry" or "physics," but give them a bottle of soap bubbles or a magnet, and watch their eyes light up!

Discovering things on their own gives kids a wonderful feeling of success. All they need is your friendly guidance, a few good ideas, and their natural curiosity. This book is full of fun ideas. It contains instructions for more than 50 simple, hands-on experiments inspired by questions from real kids. While you play together, your child will find out the answers to questions such as "How do planes fly?", "Why do lemons taste sour?", and lots of other things that children wonder about.

So get ready to enter into a science adventure.

Playfully yours,

Janice VanCleave

Before You Begin

1 ***Read the experiment completely before starting.*** When possible, practice the experiment by yourself prior to your science playtime. This increases your understanding of the topic and makes you more familiar with the procedure and the materials. If you know the experiment well, it will be easier for you to give your child instructions and answer questions. If you want to know more about the basic science behind the experiment, see Appendix B.

2 ***Select a place to work.*** The kitchen table is usually the best place for the experiments. It provides space and access to an often needed water supply.

3 ***Choose a time.*** There is no best time to play with your child, and play should be the main point when doing the experiments in this book. Select a time when you will have the fewest distrac-

tions so that you can complete the experiment. If your family has a schedule, you may allot a specific amount of time for the experiment. You may want to set an exact starting time so that the child can watch the clock and become more familiar with time. Try to schedule 5 to 10 minutes at the close of each session to have everyone clean up.

4 ***Collect supplies.*** You will have less frustration and more fun if all the materials are ready before you start. (See "Tips on Materials" in the box on the next page.)

5 ***Do not rush through the experiment.*** Follow each step carefully, and for sure and safe results, never skip steps or add your own. Safety is of the utmost importance, and it is good science technique to teach children to follow instructions when doing a science experiment.

6 ***Have fun!*** Don't worry if the child isn't "getting" the scientific principle, or if the results aren't exactly perfect. If you feel the results are too different from those described, reread the instructions and start over from step 1.

7 ***Enjoy the wonder of participating in the learning process.*** Remember, it is OK for your child not to discover the scientific explanation. For example, when you perform the experiment "Bubbly," the child may be too excited to stop blowing bubbles and listen to your explanation of why bubbles form. Don't force the child to listen. Join in the fun and make a magic moment to remember. Later, when questions about bubbles arise, you can remind the child of the fun time that you had doing the "Bubbly" experiment, then repeat the experiment, providing the explanation.

Tips on Materials

- Some experiments call for water. If you want everything to be at the worktable, you can supply water in a pitcher or soda bottle.
- Extra paper towels are always handy for accidental spills, especially if the experiment calls for liquids. A large bowl can be used for waste liquids, and the bowl can be emptied in the sink later.
- To save time, you can precut some of the materials (except string; see below).
- Do not cut string in advance, because it generally gets tangled and is difficult to separate. You and the child can measure and cut the string together.
- You may want to keep labeled shoe boxes filled with basic supplies that are used in many experiments, such as scissors, tape, marking pens, and so forth.

- The specific sizes and types of containers listed in the material lists are those used when these experiments were tested. This doesn't mean that substituting a different type of container will result in an experimental failure. Substitution of supplies should be a value judgment made after you read an experiment to determine the use of the supplies. For example, you could replace a 1-pint (500-ml) jar to mix soap bubbles with a tall drinking glass that is equal, or nearly equal, to 1 pint (500 ml).
- For large groups, multiply the supplies by the number in the group so that each person can perform the experiment individually. Some of the supplies (like glue) can be shared, so read the procedure to determine this ahead of time.

Air

Spacey

Round Up These Things

bowl, at least 4 inches (10 cm) tall and 6 inches (15 cm) in diameter
ruler
tap water
paper towel
3-ounce (90-ml) paper cup

Later You'll Need

1-gallon (1-liter) resealable plastic bag
CAUTION: Never let young children play with plastic bags on their own. Put the bag safely away after the experiment.

I wonder . . . Is there a way to catch the air?

Let's find out!

1 Fill the bowl with about 3 inches (7.5 cm) of water.

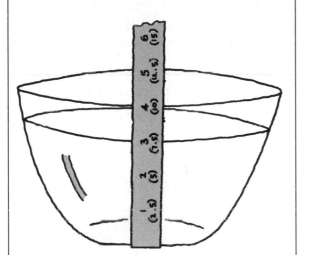

2 Crumple the paper towel into a ball and push it into the inside bottom of the cup.

3 Turn the cup upside down. The crumpled towel must remain against the bottom of the cup. If the towel moves or falls out, uncrumple it a little.

4 Hold the cup upside down. Push the cup straight down into the bowl of water until the mouth of the cup touches the bottom of the bowl.
NOTE: Do not tilt the cup.

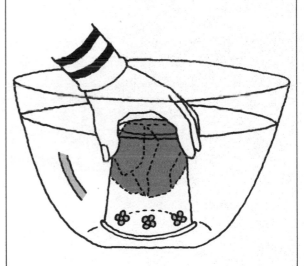

5 Lift the cup out of the water, again without tilting the cup.

6 Remove the crumpled towel from the cup and examine it. The towel will still be dry.

So Now We Know

Air is easy to catch, because it's all around you. Air fills all the empty spaces in a room. Air also fills an empty paper cup. When you put the cup in the bowl of water, the air in the cup kept the water away from the paper towel.

More Fun Things to Know and Do

Catch some air in the
resealable plastic bag by
opening the bag and moving
it through the air. Seal the
bag, then squeeze it
between your hands. You
cannot see the air inside the
bag, but you know it is
there because the bag is
inflated and it changes
shape as you push the air
around inside the bag.

Drifter

Round Up These Things

scissors
ruler
string
transparent tape
sheet of typing paper
2 small paper clips
grape-size piece of
  modeling clay

Later You'll Need

parachute and clay figure from
  original experiment
plus
grape-size piece of
  modeling clay
small paper clip

I wonder ...
What holds
up a
parachute?

Let's find
out!

1 Cut four 12-inch (30-cm) pieces of string.

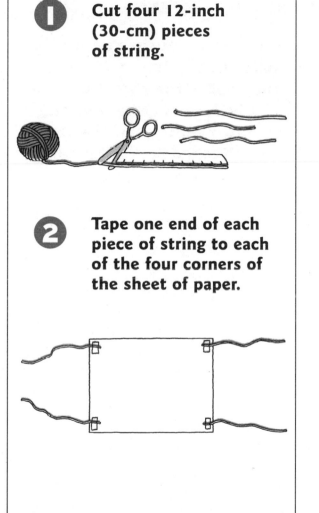

2 Tape one end of each piece of string to each of the four corners of the sheet of paper.

3 Lay the paper on a table with the tape side down. Bring the four free ends of the strings together and wrap a piece of tape around them.

4 Open a paper clip to make a hook. Tape the paper clip to the tape on the ends of the strings. You have made a parachute.

5 Shape a figure out of the clay and press it onto the other paper clip so that a small part of one end of the paper clip extends above the figure.

6 Attach the clip of the clay figure to the hook on the parachute.

7 Hold the short ends of the paper part of the parachute so that the clay figure hangs down.

8 Raise the parachute in your hands as high as possible.

9 Drop the parachute. It and the clay figure will slowly fall.

So Now We Know

Air fills and pushes up on the inside of a falling parachute. This makes the parachute fall slowly. Your clay figure floated down gently because it was attached to a parachute.

More Fun Things to Know and Do

Make a second clay figure the same size as the first one and press it onto a paper clip. The two figures should weigh about the same. Hold your paper parachute as before with its clay figure attached to the hook. At the same time, ask your helper to hold the second clay figure so that the two figures are at the same height. On the count of three, drop both clay figures and watch to determine which one hits the ground first.

Lifter

Round Up These Things

two 9-inch (23-cm) round
  balloons
scissors
ruler
thread
transparent tape
*CAUTION: Never let young chil-
dren play with deflated balloons
on their own. Put the balloons
safely away after the experiment.*

Later You'll Need

scissors
ruler
heavy string, such as kite string
2 bananas
2 apples
transparent tape
sheet of typing paper

Inflate the balloons so that they are about the same size, and knot the ends.

 Cut two 12-inch (30-cm) pieces of thread.

 Tie one end of each thread to each balloon.

 Tape the free end of each thread to the edge of a table so that the balloons hang at the same height and about 6 inches (15 cm) apart.

5 Blow as hard as you can between the hanging balloons. The balloons will move toward each other.

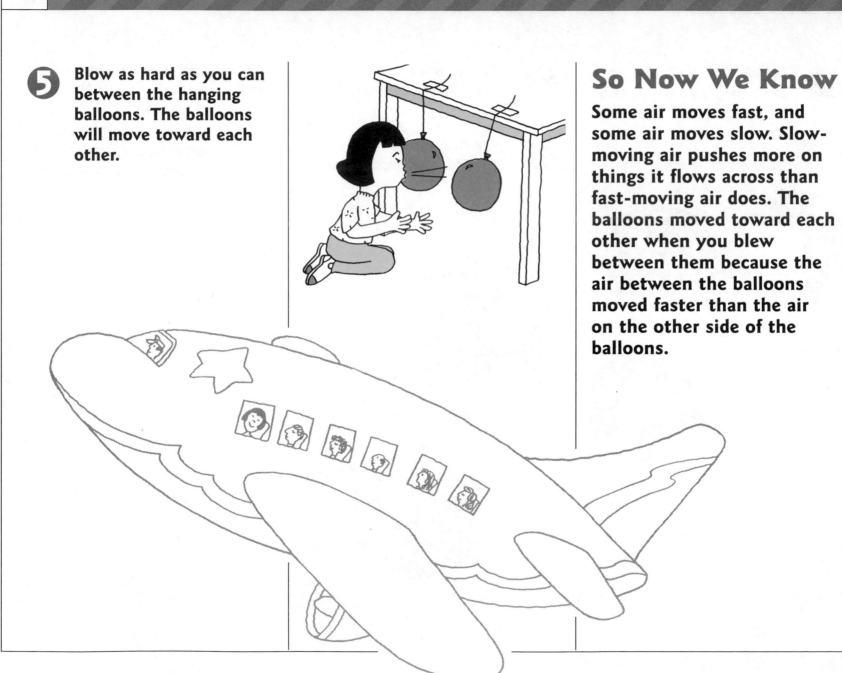

So Now We Know

Some air moves fast, and some air moves slow. Slow-moving air pushes more on things it flows across than fast-moving air does. The balloons moved toward each other when you blew between them because the air between the balloons moved faster than the air on the other side of the balloons.

More Fun Things to Know and Do

1 Balloons are very light and move easily, but heavy things will also move if the air flows fast on one side and slow on the other. Repeat the experiment twice, using heavier string, such as kite string. First tie the apples to the string, then the bananas.

2 Air flows faster across the top of airplane wings because the wings are made in a special curved shape that helps the air passing over the wings to move faster than the air passing under the wings. The greater upward push from the slower-moving air under the wings pushes the wings up, taking the rest of the plane with them.

To see how moving air makes airplane wings work, cut a 2-by-8-inch (5-by-20-cm) strip of typing paper. Hold one end of the paper against your chin, just below your bottom lip. Observe the curved shape of the paper near your chin. Blow across the top of the paper. The paper will lift.

Bubbly

Round Up These Things

1-quart (1-liter) jar
tap water
serving tray
2 teaspoons (10 ml)
 bubble bath
drinking straw

*I wonder ...
What makes
the bubbles in
bubble bath?*

*Let's find
out!*

Later You'll Need

the same materials
plus
spoon
1 cup (250 ml) tap water
1 tablespoon (15 ml) dishwashing liquid
1 tablespoon (15 ml) glycerin
 (available at a pharmacy)
bowl
plastic fly swatter

1 Fill the jar half full with water.

2 Set the jar on the tray.

3 Add the bubble bath to the water in the jar. Do not stir.

4 Insert the straw in the jar just beneath the surface of the water.

BUBBLE △ BATH

SCIENCE PROJECTS VAN

134 7912

5 Blow through the straw as hard as you can. Mounds of bubbles will form on the surface of the water. *CAUTION: Do not drink through the straw.*

So Now We Know

Bubbles are made of water, soap, and air. The bubble bath made your water soapy and stretchy. Blowing through the straw pushed air into the water, just as water splashing into your bathtub pushes air into the soapy water. The soapy water stretched around the air to make bubbles.

More Fun Things to Know and Do

1 How big can a bubble get? Like a balloon, a soap bubble gets bigger and bigger as air is added to it, because soapy water is stretchy. Too much air can pull the soapy "skin" on the outside of the bubble apart, causing the bubble to break.

- Repeat the experiment, creating a mound of bubbles in the jar.
- Take the straw out of the water and insert it into the middle of the mound of bubbles.
- Blow into the bubbles. One large bubble will form. How big a bubble can you blow?

2 Bubbles break when the water in their soapy skin dries up. An ingredient called glycerin in bubble soap keeps bubbles from drying out too quickly. Make some homemade bubble soap:

- Stir together 1 cup (250 ml) water, 1 tablespoon (15 ml) of dishwashing liquid, and 1 tablespoon (15 ml) of glycerin in the bowl.

- Place the bowl on a table outdoors and dip the fly swatter into the bubble mix.
- Swish the swatter through the air. Lots of tiny bubbles will form in the air.

Changes

Dried Out

I wonder . . .
How could I get the salt out of seawater?

SALT

Round Up These Things

1-cup (250-ml) measuring cup
tap water
2 tablespoons (30 ml) table salt
spoon
art brush
sheet of black construction paper
blow-dryer

Later You'll Need

the same materials
but
substitute 2 tablespoons
(30 ml) Epsom salts for
the table salt

Let's find out!

1 Fill the measuring cup one-fourth (63 ml) full with water.

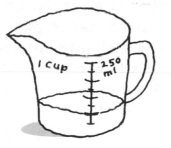

2 Add the salt to the water in the cup.

3 Stir well. The solution will look cloudy and there will be a few undissolved salt crystals in the bottom of the cup.

4 Swish the bristles of the art brush around in the saltwater so that you get a lot of salt-water on the brush.

5 Use the brush to cover the entire surface of the black paper with saltwater, rewetting the brush as often as necessary.

6 Adult Step Use the blow-dryer to dry the paper. Clear, box-shaped crystals will be stuck to the paper.

So Now We Know

You can get salt out of salt-water by making the water change into an invisible air-like material called gas. Water will change into a gas when it's heated. The blow-dryer heated the saltwater until the water was changed into a gas and was gone from the paper, and only the salt was left.

More Fun Things to Know and Do

In nature, water mixes with different salts found in soil. When the water evaporates, dry crystals are left. Different salts produce differently shaped crystals. Evaporating water from a mixture of Epsom salts and water leaves long spindles of clear, shiny crystals in starburst patterns. If the mixture is painted in the shape of a letter on a sheet of black paper, the outline of the dried crystals will be in the shape of the letter.

- Make an Epsom salts and water solution by putting 2 tablespoons (30 ml) of Epsom salts in ¼ cup (63 ml) of water and stirring.

- Swish the bristles of the art brush around in the water. Then use the brush to make a letter, one section at a time, on the black paper, rewetting the brush as each section is made.

- ADULT STEP Dry the paper with the blow-dryer.

Bouncy Blubber

Round Up These Things

1 quart (1 liter) distilled water
1 tablespoon (15 ml) borax (a water softener sold as a laundry aid)
1-quart (1-liter) jar
spoon
timer
coffee cup
4-ounce (120-ml) bottle of white school glue
bowl
cold tap water
resealable plastic bag
paper towel
marking pen
CAUTION: Keep the box of borax away from small children and do not allow them to drink the borax solution. See the warning on the box.

Later You'll Need

bouncy blubber from original experiment

1 Put the distilled water and the borax in the jar. Stir.

2 Wait 5 minutes to allow any undissolved borax to settle to the bottom of the jar.

3 Fill the cup three-fourths full with the borax solution.

4 ADULT STEP Hold the glue bottle upside down above the cup of borax, then squeeze the bottle so that a steady, thin stream of glue falls into the cup.

5 Use the spoon to keep stirring as the glue enters the cup.

6 A white stringlike mass will form and wrap around the spoon.

 7 ADULT STEP When the spoon becomes coated, stop squeezing the glue bottle.

8 With your hands, pull the white mass, which we'll call bouncy blubber, off the spoon and put it in a bowl of cold water.

9 Remove the bouncy blubber and lay it on top of the plastic bag.

10 Dry your hands with the paper towel.

11 Squeeze the bouncy blubber in your hands for about 20 to 30 seconds.

12 Shape the bouncy blubber into a ball by gently

pressing and rolling it between your hands.

13 Bounce your bouncy blubber ball on a table or on a tile floor.

14 Repeat steps 3 through 11 to make more bouncy blubber.

15 Store your bouncy blubber in the resealable bag. Label the bag **Do Not Eat** and place it in the refrigerator to prevent mold.

So Now We Know

Like a bouncy blubber ball, most balls are made of a stretchy material that always goes back to its original shape. When you bounced the bouncy blubber ball on the floor, the side of the ball that hit the floor was pushed in. But because the ball is made of stretchy material, the pushed-in side went back to its original shape and pushed against the floor, making the ball bounce.

More Fun Things to Know and Do

Balls that are to be bounced are usually round because you can control the direction that a round ball bounces. If you throw a round ball straight down, it bounces straight up. But you cannot control the direction of the bounce of a ball that is not round. Shape the bouncy blubber into other shapes, such as a cube or a pyramid. Compare the bounciness of the different shapes.

I wonder how a square ball would bounce.

Mixers

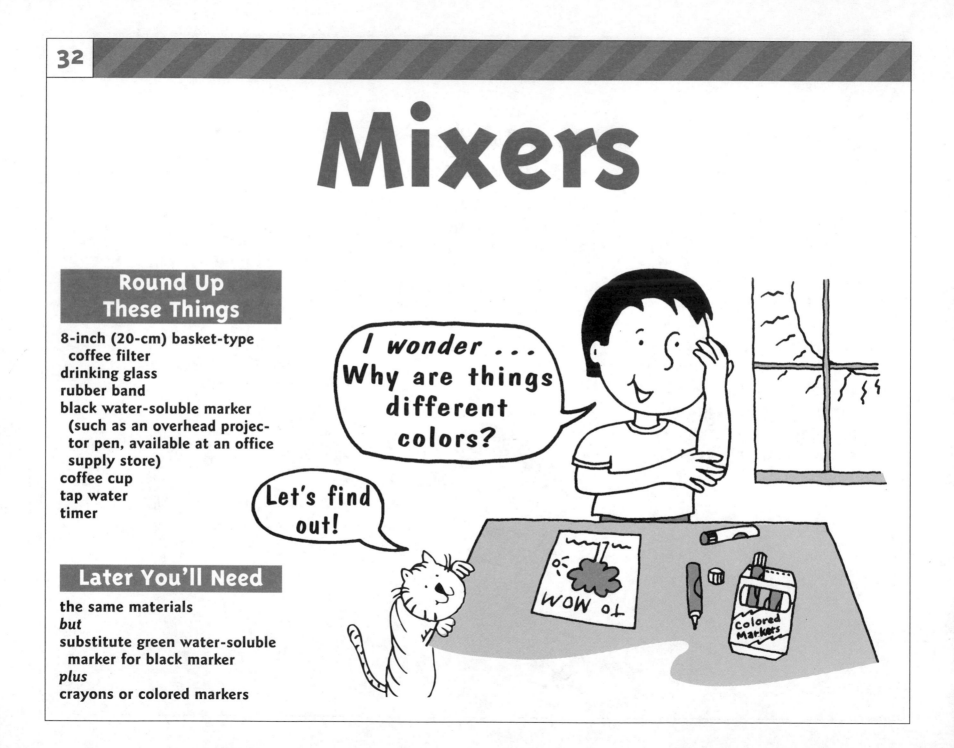

Round Up These Things

8-inch (20-cm) basket-type
  coffee filter
drinking glass
rubber band
black water-soluble marker
  (such as an overhead projec-
  tor pen, available at an office
  supply store)
coffee cup
tap water
timer

Later You'll Need

the same materials
but
substitute green water-soluble
  marker for black marker
plus
crayons or colored markers

1 Stretch the coffee filter over the mouth of the glass.

2 Use the rubber band to hold the filter tightly against the glass.

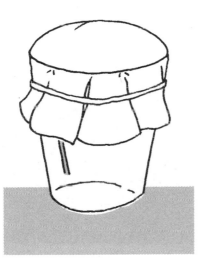

3 Use the black marker to draw a small flower in the center of the filter.

4 Fill the cup with water.

5 Wet the tip of one finger in the water, then touch the center of the flower with the wet fingertip.

6 Wet your fingertip again and touch the center of one petal.

Repeat step 6 for each petal.

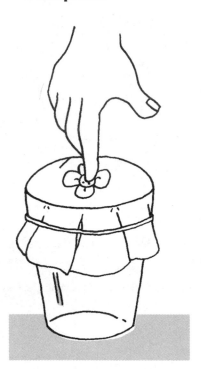

 Without tilting the glass, watch the flower change. (Tilting the glass makes the water on the filter move around and spoils the flower design.)

9 **When no further changes are seen, repeat steps 5 through 8 one more time.**

10 **Wait 5 to 10 minutes for the filter to dry.**

11 **Remove the rubber band and spread the filter flat. The black ink will be separated into colors. Keep the filter for the second experiment in "More Fun Things to Know and Do."**

So Now We Know

Black is a combination of lots of different colors. When water is added to a mark of black ink on paper, the colors separate and become visible. That is how you were able to see the multicolored design on the filter.

More Fun Things to Know and Do

I wonder what would happen if I use a different color.

1 Other colors of ink also separate on paper when wet; for example, green separates into blue and yellow. Repeat the experiment, using the green water-soluble marker.

2 The things you see reflect only some of the rainbow colors in light. A plant is green because it reflects the green part of light. An apple is red because it reflects the red part of light.

Use one of your dried designs and crayons or colored markers to make a colorful picture. Add stems and leaves to the design, then complete the picture by adding grass, clouds, birds, and the sun.

Note all the different colors of light that are reflected by the colored substances in each crayon or marker.

Play Clay

Round Up These Things

1 cup (250 ml) flour
½ cup (125 ml) table salt
2 tablespoons (30 ml) cream
  of tartar
2-quart (2-liter) bowl
spoon
¾ cup (188 ml) tap water
saucepan
oven mitt
1 tablespoon (15 ml) cooking oil
timer
1-quart (1-liter) resealable
  plastic bag

Later You'll Need

the same materials
plus
food coloring
*NOTE: Even though the play clay is
  nontoxic, it should not be eaten
  because it contains a large amount
  of salt.*

1. Put the flour, salt, and cream of tartar in the bowl.

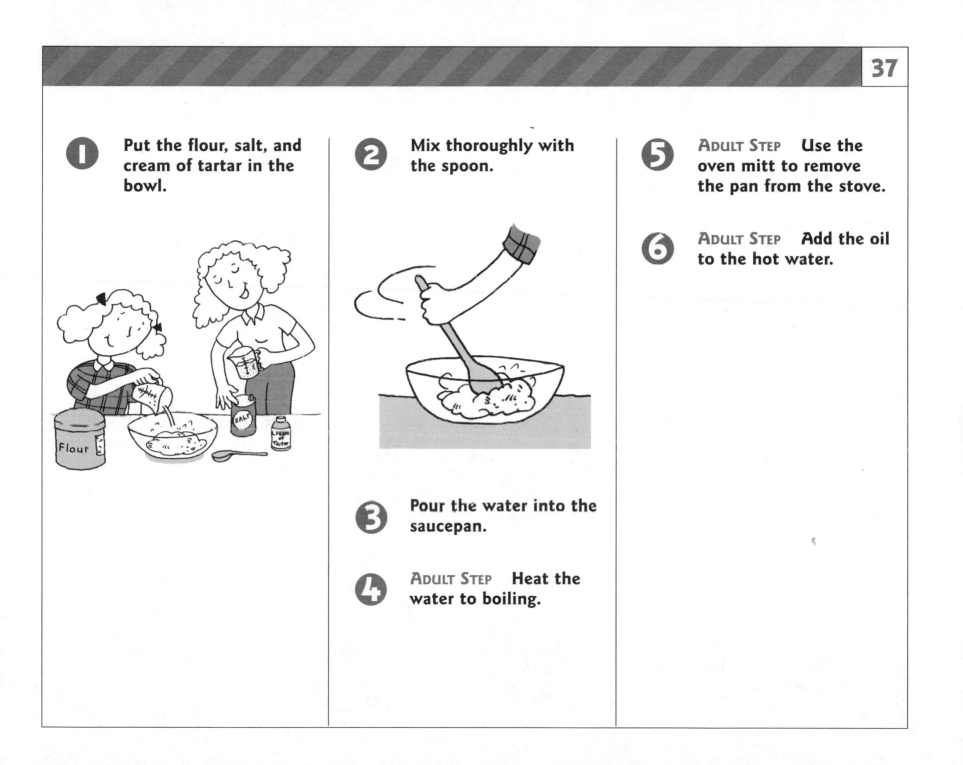

2. Mix thoroughly with the spoon.

3. Pour the water into the saucepan.

4. ADULT STEP   Heat the water to boiling.

5. ADULT STEP   Use the oven mitt to remove the pan from the stove.

6. ADULT STEP   Add the oil to the hot water.

7 **ADULT STEP** Slowly pour the hot liquid into the bowl that contains the flour mixture, stirring as the liquid is being added.

8 Wait 5 minutes or until the mixture is cool enough to handle. Then, thoroughly mix the play clay by squeezing it between your hands.

9 Mold the play clay into different shapes, such as people, dinosaurs, or flowers.

10 Store the clay in the resealable bag.

So Now We Know

When you mix things together and heat them, they often turn into something else. Flour, salt, water, and oil in certain amounts make play clay (which you shouldn't eat because of the high amount of salt), but flour, sugar, milk, and oil in other amounts make cookies!

More Fun Things to Know and Do

The clay can be colored by adding food coloring to the hot liquid before adding the liquid to the flour mixture. Repeat the experiment, using about 20 drops of food coloring.

Pucker Up

Round Up These Things

2 tablespoons (30 ml) Red Cabbage
Juice Indicator (see Appendix A)
saucer
1 teaspoon (5 ml) lemon juice
spoon

Later You'll Need

antacid tablet
paper cup or any other small container
2 tablespoons (30 ml) tap water
timer
measuring spoons
4 tablespoons (60 ml) Red Cabbage
Juice Indicator (see Appendix A)
2 saucers
eyedropper
1 teaspoon (5 ml) lemon juice
CAUTION: *If splashed on your skin, even weak acids, such as lemon juice, vinegar, or tomato juice, can cause stinging pain and damage to your skin. While this damage is minor with weak acids, you should avoid getting them on your skin. If acids do splash on you, immediately wash them off with cold water.*

I wonder . . . Why do lemons taste sour?

Let's find out!

1 Put the Red Cabbage Juice Indicator in the saucer.

2 Add the lemon juice to the indicator. Stir.

So Now We Know

Lemons taste sour because they contain acid. Acid does other things, too. It makes some foods, such as red cabbage juice, change color. We know that there is acid in something if it turns red cabbage juice from purple to a color that ranges from pink to red.

More Fun Things to Know and Do

1 Antacid tablets are basic. A base is a chemical that is the opposite of an acid. Bases taste bitter and turn red cabbage juice from purple to a color that ranges from blue to green.

To watch this happen:

- Place the antacid tablet in the cup and add 2 tablespoons (30 ml) of water.

- Allow the cup to sit for 3 to 5 minutes so that the tablet partially dissolves in the water.

- Put 2 tablespoons (30 ml) of Red Cabbage Juice Indicator in one of the saucers, then add 1 teaspoon (5 ml) of the antacid liquid from the cup. Stir.

- Watch as the red cabbage juice turns blue to green, the color range of bases.

 2 When acids and bases are mixed together, they cancel each other, resulting in a neutral chemical.

To make a neutral chemical:

- Mix together 1 teaspoon (5 ml) of antacid liquid from the cup and 2 tablespoons (30 ml) of Red Cabbage Juice Indicator in the other saucer.

- Use the eyedropper to add a few drops of lemon juice to the liquid in the saucer. Stir.

- Continue to add the lemon juice a few drops at a time, stirring after each addition, until the liquid in the saucer is purple, the color of neutral solutions.

Shiny Coins

Round Up These Things

½ cup (125 ml) white vinegar
¼ teaspoon (1.25 ml) table salt
measuring cup
spoon
8 dull copper pennies
small bowl
timer
coffee cup
tap water
paper

I wonder ... Why are some pennies shinier than others?

Later You'll Need

3 uncleaned copper pennies and bowl of vinegar and salt solution from original experiment
plus
new shiny paper clip
spoon
CAUTION: If splashed on your skin, even weak acids, such as lemon juice, vinegar, or tomato juice, can cause stinging pain and damage to your skin. While this damage is minor with weak acids, you should avoid getting them on your skin. If acids do splash on you, immediately wash them off with cold water.

Let's find out!

1 Put the vinegar and the salt in the measuring cup. Stir.

2 Lay 5 of the pennies flat in the bowl. They may touch each other but should not be stacked on top of each other.

3 Pour the vinegar and salt solution into the bowl.

4 Watch the pennies change from a dull color to a shiny copper color.

5 In 3 to 5 minutes, use the spoon to transfer the pennies from the bowl to the coffee cup. Keep the bowl of vinegar and salt solution for the experiment in "More Fun Things to Know and Do."

6 Fill the cup with water to rinse the vinegar off the coins.

7 Dry the coins with the paper towel.

8 Compare the cleaned pennies with those that were not cleaned. The cleaned coins will be shiny and the uncleaned coins will be dull.

So Now We Know

New pennies are shiny. As pennies get older, they start to look dull. This happens when a gas in the air combines with the metal in the pennies. When you soaked the pennies in the vinegar and salt solution, they became shiny again.

More Fun Things to Know and Do

Copper is one of the metals used to make pennies. The vinegar and salt solution removed bits of copper molecules at the same time that it removed the dull color from the pennies. The copper molecules in the solution are so small that they are invisible, but they will stick to an object made of certain metals, such as a paper clip, and become visible.

To see this happen:

- Place the 3 uncleaned pennies in the bowl of vinegar and salt solution saved from the experiment.

- Add the new, shiny paper clip to the bowl.

- Leave the bowl undisturbed overnight. A thin layer of copper will develop over the surface of the paper clip.

- Use the spoon to remove the paper clip and allow it to air-dry. Do not rub the paper clip or else you will remove the copper.

Magnets

Stickers

Round Up These Things

refrigerator magnet (a disk magnet used in the experiment "North Seekers" will work)
sheet of paper
pencil
ruler
scissors
rubber band
3 to 4 small metal paper clips

Later You'll Need

pencil
sheet of typing paper
ruler
scissors
crayons
transparent tape
3 to 5 small metal paper clips
shoe box
magnet

1 Lay the magnet on the paper.

2 Draw a rectangle on the paper that is about the same width as the magnet and about 2 inches (5 cm) longer.

3 Cut out the rectangle from the paper.

4 Hold the magnet close to, but not touching, the paper rectangle. Observe whether the paper moves toward the magnet. The paper does not move, which means that the paper is not attracted to the magnet.

5 Wrap the paper rectangle around the magnet and secure it with the rubber band.

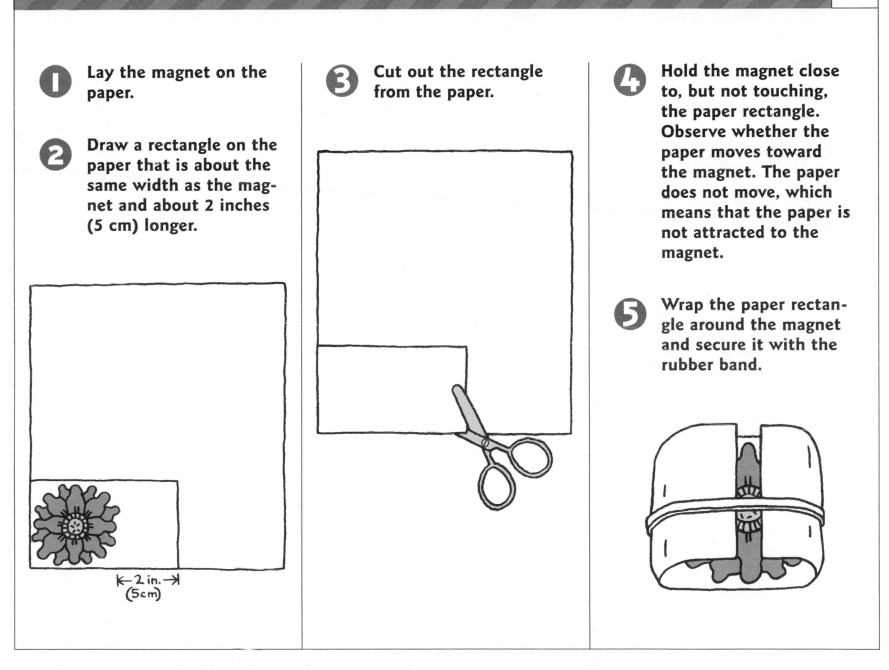

←2 in.→
(5cm)

6 Place the paper clips on a nonmetal table.

7 Hold the paper-wrapped magnet about 6 inches (15 cm) above the paper clips.

8 Slowly lower the magnet. The paper clips will move toward the magnet. This means that the power of the magnet moves through the paper and attracts the metal paper clips.

So Now We Know

Magnets have a force that pulls them toward metal things, such as paper clips and refrigerators. This force works even through paper! That's why your drawings stay stuck to the refrigerator.

More Fun Things to Know and Do

When a magnet moves, its magnetic force moves with it. A paper clip attracted to a magnet through a sheet of paper will move where the magnet moves. You can use a magnet this way to put on a puppet show.

- Draw and cut out 3 to 5 paper figures, similar to the one shown here. Use crayons to draw faces and clothes on the figures.

- Tape a paper clip to the base of each figure. Remember that you want the figure to be as light as possible, so don't use too much tape.

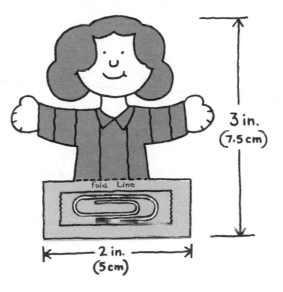

3 in. (7.5 cm)

2 in. (5 cm)

Fold Line

- Fold the base under along the fold line.

- Use an open shoe box for a stage. Stand the shoe box so that its open end faces you.

- Place the paper figures on top of the box. Hold the magnet inside the box under one of the figures. Move the figure by moving the magnet.

North Seekers

Round Up These Things

masking tape
sheet of paper
compass
marking pen
6-inch (15-cm) piece of string
2 disk magnets of equal size

Later You'll Need

disk magnet from original experiment
plus
small paper clip
8-inch (20-cm) piece of thread
timer
pencil
tall, clear drinking glass
NOTE: Never touch a compass with a magnet. Touching a compass with a strong magnet can change the polarity of the compass needle, causing the pole marked north to become a south pole and all directions to be reversed.

1 Tape the sheet of paper to the top of a non-metal table. Be sure that there are no magnetic materials on or near the table.

2 Place the compass in the center of the paper and watch the compass needle move. Slowly rotate the compass until the colored part of the compass needle points to the N on the compass.

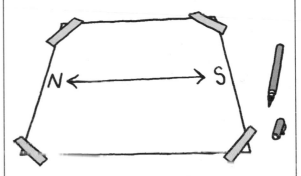

3 Use the marking pen to make a mark on the paper at the north and south compass points.

4 Remove the compass.

5 Label the directions N and S with the pen. Draw an arrow connecting the two points. You have made a paper compass.

6 Tape the string to the rounded edge of one of the disk magnets. Keep the other magnet away from the table.

 7 Holding the free end of the string, hang the magnet over the paper compass until the magnet's flat sides point steadily in a north-to-south direction.

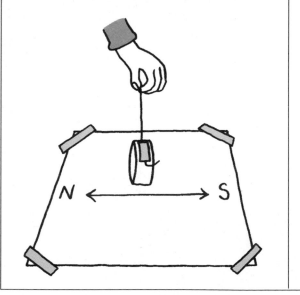

8 Use the tape and the marking pen to label the side of the magnet that points north with a large dot and the side that points south with a large X.

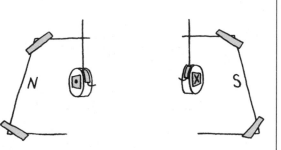

9 Remove the string from the magnet.

10 Repeat steps 6 through 9 to label the flat sides of the second magnet. Keep these magnets for the experiment "Pushers."

So Now We Know

The needle inside a compass is a little magnet that can swing around. One end of the needle always points north. The hanging disk magnet also swung around so that one side pointed north. Every magnet has a north end and a south end. The dots mark the north end of each magnet, and the X marks their south end.

More Fun Things to Know and Do

A paper clip can be magnetized by laying it on top of a magnet. This magnetized paper clip will point north if it is hung from a thread.

To see this happen:

- Clip the paper clip to one end of the 8-inch (20-cm) piece of thread.

- Lay the narrow end of the paper clip across the X on the magnet.

- After about 2 minutes, remove the paper clip from the magnet and tie the free end of the thread to the center of the pencil. The narrow end of the magnetized paper clip is the north end.

- Lay the pencil across the mouth of the glass so that the paper clip is suspended in the glass and is protected from air currents. Watch what happens to the paper clip.

Pushers

Round Up These Things

2 labeled disk magnets from the experiment "North Seekers"

Later You'll Need

12-inch (30-cm) piece of string
2 small bar magnets
masking tape
2 disk magnets with holes in their centers (available at hobby, craft, or teaching supply stores)
pencil thin enough to slip easily through the holes in the magnets

I wonder ... Why do magnets sometimes push each other away?

Let's find out!

1 Stand one of the magnets on edge on a non-metal table.

2 Hold the other magnet near, but not touching, the magnet on the table so that the X side of the magnet in your hand and the X side of the magnet on the table face you. The magnet on the table will roll away from the magnet in your hand.

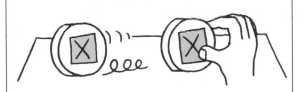

3 Turn the magnet in your hand around so that the side with the large dot faces you. Hold it close to, but not touching, the magnet on the table. The magnet on the table will roll toward the magnet in your hand.

So Now We Know

Magnets push away from each other when the north end of one faces the north end of the other, or when the south end of one faces the south end of the other. That is why the disk magnet on the table rolled away from

the magnet in your hand. But when the south end of one magnet faces the north end of another magnet, the magnets pull toward each other. That is why the disk magnet on the table rolled toward the magnet in your hand.

More Fun Things to Know and Do

1. The ends of bar magnets push away from or pull toward each other, just as the ends of disk magnets do.

- Tie the string around the middle of one of the bar magnets.

- Tape the free end of the string to the edge of a nonmetal table so that the magnet hangs horizontally.

- Hold the second bar magnet in your hand so that one end is near, but not touching, one end of the hanging magnet. Observe the movement of the hanging magnet.

- Turn the magnet in your hand around so that the ends face the other way, and hold it near the same end of the hanging magnet, as before. Again, observe the movement of the hanging magnet.

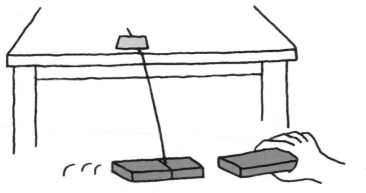

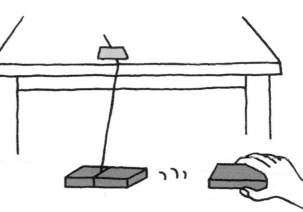

2 The push between magnets can be great enough to float a magnet in the air. The floating magnet can be raised and lowered without touching it.

- Place the pencil through the holes in the 2 disk magnets. If the magnets stick together, remove one of the magnets and turn it over.

- Ask a helper to hold the pencil upright as you raise and lower the bottom magnet.

- Observe the movement of the upper magnet.

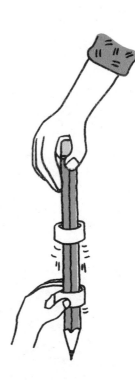

Forces

Soakers

Round Up These Things

plate
2-ply white paper towel
3-ounce (90-ml) paper cup
tap water
red food coloring
spoon
eyedropper

Later You'll Need

red, yellow, and blue food coloring
six to ten 3-ounce (90-ml)
   paper cups
6 to 10 paper towels of the
   same brand
colored water from original
   experiment
plus
saucer
cookie sheet
scissors
ruler
3 or more paper towels, each a
   different brand
timer

1 Set the plate on a table and cover the plate with the paper towel.

2 Fill the paper cup half full with water.

3 Add 10 drops of food coloring to the water. Stir.

4 Fill the eyedropper with the colored water.

5 Release a drop of colored water onto the paper towel. The colored water will move outward in different directions.

Repeat step 5 four or more times, placing the drops in different areas of the paper towel. Keep the remaining colored water for the second experiment in "More Fun Things to Know and Do."

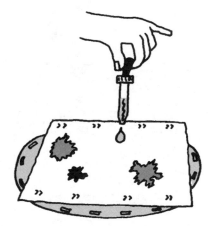

So Now We Know

Water sticks to paper. Paper towels soak up water because they are made of lots of little bits of paper with tiny spaces between the bits that hold the water. The water moves from bit to bit, filling the spaces. Adding food coloring to the water made the movement of the water more visible.

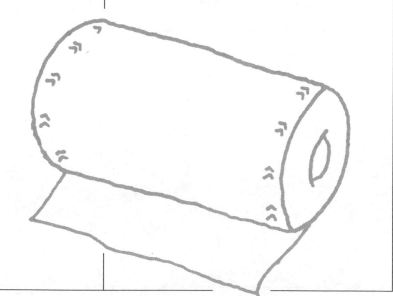

More Fun Things to Know and Do

1 How would different colors soak into a paper towel? Repeat the experiment, mixing red, yellow, and blue food coloring to make orange, purple, and green coloring for the water. Use the following chart to produce these colors.

Color Combination (5 drops of each)	Resulting Color
yellow + red	orange
red + blue	purple
blue + yellow	green

NOTE: Vary the number of drops of each color to make other tints and shades of the resulting colors.

Mix each color in a separate cup and test it on a separate paper towel, using the same brand of paper towel for each color. Rinse the eyedropper after each test.

2 Different brands of paper towels soak up different amounts of water. Test different brands to decide which soaks up the most water.

- Place the saucer at one end of the cookie sheet and fill it with the colored water saved from the original experiment.

- Cut a 2-inch (5-cm) strip from each paper towel.

- Place one end of each strip in the colored water. Lay the other end of each strip on the cookie sheet.

- Wait 3 to 5 minutes or until the colored water stops moving through the strips. Did the water travel farther through one of the strips?

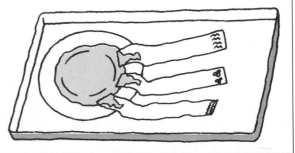

Roly-Poly

Round Up These Things

baby powder
cookie sheet
coffee can or other 6-inch
 (15-cm)-tall can
masking tape
¼ cup (63 ml) tap water
red food coloring
coffee cup
spoon
eyedropper

Later You'll Need

the same materials
except
coffee can
masking tape
plus
ruler

I wonder . . . Why do things roll downhill?

Let's find out!

Spread a thin layer of baby powder over the surface of the cookie sheet.

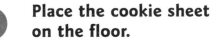 Place the cookie sheet on the floor.

 Raise one end of the cookie sheet and rest it on the rim of the coffee can.

4 Secure the cookie sheet to the can with tape.

5 Put the water and 10 drops of food coloring in the cup. Stir.

 Fill the eyedropper with colored water.

7 Practice squeezing drops of colored water back into the cup until you can easily squeeze one drop at a time.

8 Sitting next to the raised end of the powdered cookie sheet, hold the eyedropper just above, but not touching, the raised end of the cookie sheet.

Squeeze out 1 drop of colored water and watch it roll down the powdered cookie sheet. It will become covered with powder and form a round rolling object that we'll call a roly-poly.

 Squeeze out another drop of colored water and watch it roll down the cookie sheet. If it follows the path of the first roly-poly, they will either stack on top of each other at the bottom of the cookie sheet or collide and join to form a single, larger roly-poly.

So Now We Know

Gravity is the force that makes things fall to the ground. It also makes round things such as balls and bike wheels roll downhill. That is why your roly-poly rolled down the cookie sheet.

More Fun Things to Know and Do

The steeper the hill, the faster a round object rolls down it. The speed of the roly-polies can be increased by increasing the height of the raised end of the cookie sheet.

Repeat the experiment twice, asking a helper to raise the end of the cookie sheet, first to a height of about 8 inches (20 cm) above the floor, then to a height of about 12 inches (30 cm).

Floater

Round Up These Things

2-quart (2-liter) bowl
cold tap water
2 walnut-size pieces of
  modeling clay

Later You'll Need

two 1-quart (1-liter) jars
cold tap water
6 to 9 tablespoons (90 to
  135 ml) table salt
2 small uncooked eggs
  of equal size
spoon

I wonder ... Why do boats float?

Let's find out!

1 Fill the bowl three-fourths full with cold tap water.

2 Shape one piece of clay into a ball by rolling it around between the palms of your hands.

3 Carefully place the clay ball on the surface of the water in the bowl. The ball will sink.

4 Remove the clay ball from the water and set it aside.

5 Shape the second piece of clay so that it looks like a boat. Make the bottom of the boat as large as possible and the sides short.
NOTE: Young children may need some assistance in shaping the boat.

6 Gently place the clay boat on the surface of the water in the bowl. The boat will float.

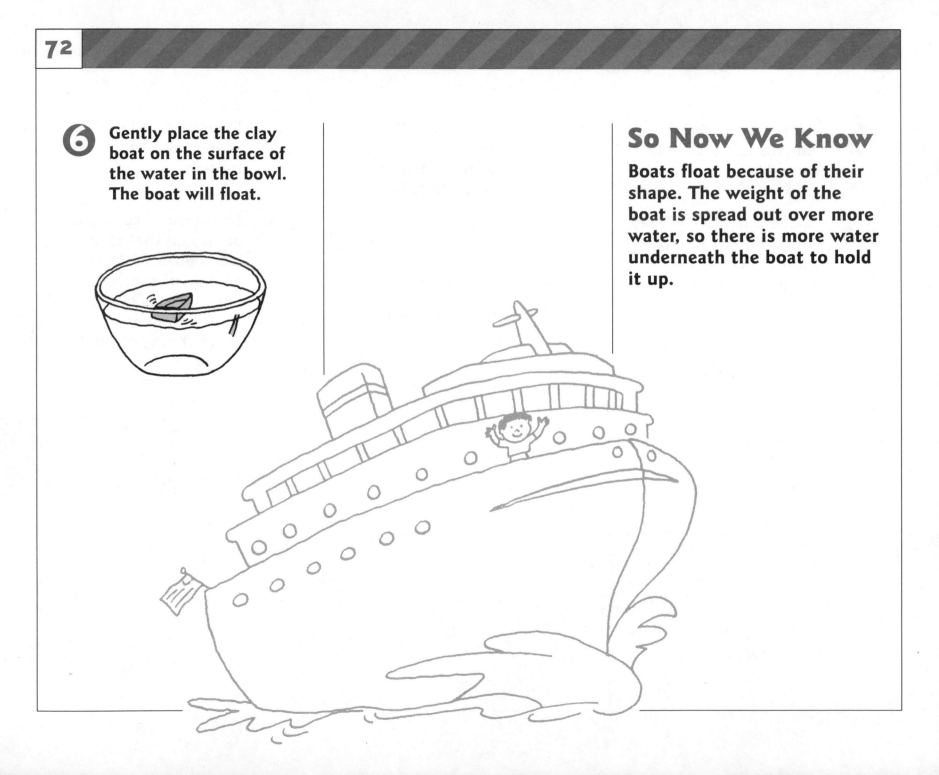

So Now We Know

Boats float because of their shape. The weight of the boat is spread out over more water, so there is more water underneath the boat to hold it up.

More Fun Things to Know and Do

Boats float better in the saltwater of oceans than in the freshwater of rivers and lakes, because saltwater weighs more and pushes up on objects more.

- Fill each jar half full with water.

- Stir 6 tablespoons (90 ml) of salt into one of the jars of water.

- Set one of the eggs on the spoon, tilt one of the jars, and gently lower the egg into the jar.

- Place the other egg in the second jar. Observe how high each egg floats.

NOTE: *Since the weight of eggs varies, you might need to add more salt to make the egg in the saltwater float near the surface.*

Breakable?

Round Up These Things

small uncooked egg
large bowl
*CAUTION: Always
wash your hands
after touching an
uncooked egg. It
may contain
harmful bacteria.*

Later You'll Need

egg from original experiment
plus
3 more uncooked eggs
metal spoon
tap water
paper towel
masking tape
nail scissors
4 to 6 books
timer

I wonder ...
Why don't eggs
break under
a chicken?

Let's CLUCK CLUCK
find out!

Hold the egg length-wise in the palm of your hand so that one of the rounded ends points toward your fingers.
NOTE: Don't wear rings.

 Hold your hand over the bowl. (This is just in case you are extra strong or there is a small crack in the eggshell and the egg breaks.)

3 Using only the hand that holds the egg, squeeze the egg as hard as you can. Unless you are very strong, the egg will not break.

So Now We Know

Eggs break easily when you hit them against a hard surface. But it's hard to break an egg just by squeezing it. That's because of the dome shape of the eggshell. The weight of the chicken's body is spread out over the eggshell, so the chicken's body doesn't push very hard in any one place.

I wonder what would happen if I hold the egg sideways.

More Fun Things to Know and Do

 Even if you hold the egg sideways, it will not break. Repeat the experiment, holding the egg sideways in your hand.

Because of an eggshell's strength, its dome shape is imitated by building designers. Test the strength of an eggshell the next time you scramble eggs.

- Use the edge of the spoon to carefully break off the small end of 4 eggs. If any cracks develop in the shell, discard the shell and use another.

- Shake out the contents of each egg and rinse the inside of the eggshells with water. Carefully dry the outside of the shells with a paper towel.

- Wrap a piece of masking tape around the center of each shell, then use the nail scissors to cut away the jagged edges of the shell from around the tape.

- Place the shells, open end down, in a rectangular array on a table. Place one of the books on top of the shells, and adjust the position of the shells so that one shell is under each corner of the book.

- Carefully add the other books, one at a time, to the book on top of the eggshells, waiting 15 seconds before adding each book. The number of books it takes to crack the eggshells will depend on the total weight of the books.

Buckle Up

Round Up These Things

4-by-12-inch (10-by-30-cm) piece of stiff cardboard (size is not critical)
book, about 1 inch (2.5 cm) thick
masking tape
pencil
walnut-size piece of modeling clay
small toy car
12-inch (30-cm) piece of ¼-inch (0.6-cm) ribbon (or any narrow ribbon)

Later You'll Need

the same materials
plus
another book about 1 inch (2.5 cm) thick

I wonder . . . Why do I have to wear a seat belt?

Let's find out!

Place one end of the cardboard on the edge of the book.

 Tape the other end of the cardboard to a table.

3 Tape the pencil to the table about two toy-car lengths from the taped end of the cardboard.

4 Make a clay figure shaped like a snowman.

5 Flatten the bottom of the clay figure and gently rest it on the hood of the toy car. Do not press the clay onto the car.

6 Position the car and clay figure at the raised end of the cardboard.

7 Release the car and watch it roll down the cardboard and collide into the pencil. The car will stop, but the clay figure will sail through the air.

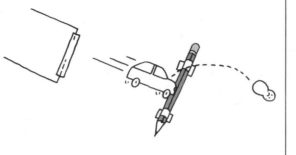

8 Use the ribbon to tie the clay figure to the car, then repeat steps 6 and 7. The clay figure will stay on the car.

So Now We Know

Moving objects continue to move forward until something stops them. The seat belt, like the ribbon around the clay figure, keeps you from getting hurt when a car suddenly stops. If you are wearing a seat belt, then the seat belt stops you. If you are not wearing a seat belt, then you keep going until something like the dashboard or the front seat stops you.

More Fun Things to Know and Do

When riding in a car, you, like the clay figure, are moving at the same speed as the car. The toy car will reach a faster speed if the cardboard is raised higher. If the clay figure is not secured to the car with ribbon, the figure will fly farther through the air.

Raise the cardboard by placing the second book on top of the first one. Repeat the experiment, noticing how far away from the pencil the figure lands.

Changing

Round Up These Things

index card
walnut-size piece of modeling clay
pencil with eraser
flashlight
ruler

Later You'll Need

spring tension rod that extends 28
  to 48 inches (70 to 120 cm)
white sheet
4 large safety pins
desk lamp or lamp without a shade
yardstick (meterstick)

1 Lay the index card on a table.

 2 Place the piece of modeling clay on the card.

3 Stand the pencil upright, eraser end up, in the clay.

 4 Turn the flashlight on.

5 Darken the room.

6 Hold the flashlight so that it is to one side of the pencil and about 4 inches (10 cm) from the eraser. Notice the length of the shadow.

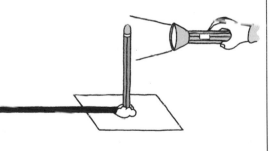

7 Hold the flashlight so that it is at an angle to the eraser and the same distance away as in step 6. The shadow will be shorter.

Hold the flashlight so that it is directly above the eraser and the same distance away as in step 6. Little or no shadow will be produced.

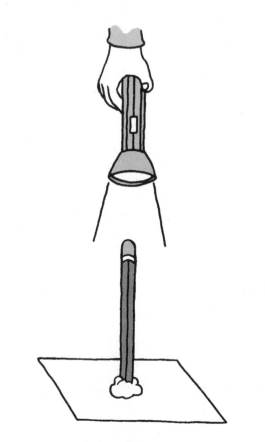

So Now We Know

Shadows change size as the position of the light that makes them changes. Your shadow appears when your body gets between the sun and the ground. When the sun, like the flashlight, is high overhead, the shadow is short. When the sun is low in the sky, the shadow is long.

More Fun Things to Know and Do

1 Light travels in a straight line and cannot bend around materials, so shadows have the same shape as the object that blocks the light. You can put on an animal-shadow show by positioning your hands and fingers so that they block light and create shadows in the shape of animals.

• Place the spring tension rod across an open doorway.

• Hang the white sheet by lapping it over the rod and securing with the safety pins. This will be your screen.

- Place the lamp about 2 yards (2 m) from the screen.

- Turn on the lamp, then darken the room.

- Hold your hands between the lamp and the screen so that your hands are about 6 inches (15 cm) from the screen.

- Position your fingers to make the animal shadows shown. Experiment to make other animal shadows.

2 The closer an object is to the light, the more light the object blocks. You can change the size of your animal shadows by changing your distance from the lamp. To produce a larger shadow on the screen, hold your hands closer to the lamp. To make a smaller shadow, stand farther from the lamp. *CAUTION: Do not hold your hands closer than 6 inches (15 cm) from the lamp. The heat from the bulb could burn your skin.*

Rainbows

Round Up These Things

garden hose
spray nozzle (optional)

Later You'll Need

1-quart (1-liter) glass jar
tap water
sheet of typing paper

Turn the water on and adjust the nozzle on the hose so that it sprays a fine mist of water. *NOTE: If you don't have a spray nozzle, you can get the same effect by holding your thumb partially over the opening of the hose.*

 Standing with the sun behind you, hold the hose so that the water sprays into the air in front of you. Move the spray from side to side until you see a rainbow in the mist.

CAUTION: Never look directly at the sun, because doing so can permanently damage your eyes.

So Now We Know

Rainbows happen when sunlight passes through water drops. The light is separated into the seven rainbow colors: red, orange, yellow, green, blue, indigo, and violet.

More Fun Things to Know and Do

Light passing through a glass container of water will separate into rainbow colors.

- Fill the jar with water.

- Place the jar indoors on a window ledge or table edge near a window. The sun must be shining directly in the window.

- Place the sheet of white paper on the shadow of the jar on the floor. Watch the rainbow appear on the paper.

Sound

Musical Glasses

I wonder ... How do chimes make music?

Let's find out!

Round Up These Things

tall drinking glass made of plain, not rippled, glass
NOTE: The thinner the glass, the better the experiment works.
wooden spoon or pencil
2-cup (500-ml) measuring cup or small pitcher
tap water

Later You'll Need

8 long-stemmed water glasses or other drinking glasses
tap water
wooden spoon or pencil

1 Stand the glass on a table.

2 Use the spoon to gently tap the side of the glass near its rim. *CAUTION: Be careful not to hit the glass hard enough to break it.*

3 Fill the measuring cup with water.

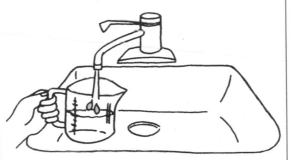

4 Continue to tap against the glass, as a helper slowly pours the water from the cup into the glass.

5 Observe the sound made as the water level rises in the glass. The sound will become lower as more water is added.

6 Look for any movement in the glass as you tap it again. A sound is heard, but you cannot see the glass shake.

7 Tap the glass again and look at the surface of the water. The water will shake. Even though you cannot see the glass shake, it does, causing the water to shake, too.

So Now We Know

Chimes make music when the wind pushes them into each other. When one chime bangs into another, both chimes shake a little. This shaking makes the sound you hear. You hear the sound because sound waves move from the chimes through the air to your ears. When you tapped the glass of water, it also shook and made a sound.

More Fun Things to Know and Do

You can make a musical instrument out of glasses by putting different amounts of water in each. The more water in a glass, the lower the musical note produced.

- Fill the first glass as much as possible with water.

- Put a little less water in the next glass.

- Continue putting less water in each glass. The eighth glass should have only a little water.

- Try to play a song by tapping on the glasses. (You may need to add or remove water to tune the instrument so that it sounds right.)

String Telephone

Round Up These Things

pencil
9-ounce (270-ml) paper cup
9-foot (2.7-m) string
paper clip

Later You'll Need

pencil
four 9-ounce (270-ml) paper cups
two 9-yard (8-m) strings
4 paper clips
3 helpers

ADULT STEP Use the pencil to make a small hole in the bottom of the cup.

 Thread the end of the string through the hole and into the cup.

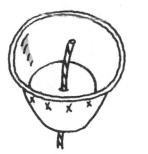

 Knot the end of the string. To keep the knot from pulling through the hole, attach the paper clip to the string between the knot and the cup.

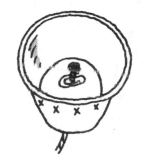

 Tie the free end of the string to a doorknob.

Walk away from the door until the string is taut.

Hold the cup to your ear while a helper gently strums, rubs, then blows on the string near the doorknob. You will hear the sounds loud and clear in the cup.

7 Trade places with your helper and repeat steps 5 and 6.

So Now We Know

In telephones that have wires, the sound travels through the wire from one telephone to another. In your string telephone, the sound traveled through a string from one place to another.

More Fun Things to Know and Do

1 Telephones send the sound of voices. A two-cup string telephone can also send voice sounds. Make another telephone, using 2 cups and one of the longer strings.

- Attach a cup to each end of the string. Take the string telephone outside.

- Ask your helper to hold one cup while you hold the other.

- Walk away from your helper until the string is taut between you.

- Take turns with your helper as one person speaks into one cup and the other listens through the other cup.

2 The sound in the string will be sent to anything the string touches. If the strings of two string telephones cross each other, three people will hear the voice of the person speaking.

- Make another two-cup telephone as in the previous experiment.

- Have two helpers (A and B) hold the cups of one telephone and walk away from each other until the string is taut between them.

- Ask a third helper (C) to help you (D) wrap the middle of the string of the other telephone once around the middle of the first telephone's string.

- Walk away from each other until the string of the second telephone is taut. Take turns speaking into the cups.

Musical Teeth

1 Place one end of the craft stick between your teeth.

2 Gently rub your finger against the other end of the stick. You will hear a loud rubbing sound.

3 Hold the stick in one hand, and with the finger of your other hand, gently rub the other end of the stick. You will hear a low rubbing sound or no sound at all.

So Now We Know

Sounds that travel through air aren't as loud as sounds that travel through solids. Most of the noise you make when you chew is heard only by you. This is because the sound goes through the bones in your head right to your ears, not into the air.

More Fun Things to Know and Do

1. Bells and chimes are made of metal because metals make sounds easily. A wire clothes hanger makes a sound like chimes.

- Wrap one end of the string around one finger of each hand.

- Hang the clothes hanger on the string so that it hangs freely.

- Ask your helper to tap the hanger several times with the spoon.

- Lean forward slightly so that the hanger does not touch your body.

- Ask your helper to tap the hanger several times with the spoon.

2 The sound of your clothes hanger chimes can be made louder if the sounds travel to your ear through a solid.

- With the strings wrapped around your two fingers as before, place your fingertips just inside your ears, being careful not to poke into your ears.

Electricity

Attractive

I wonder . . . Why does my hair stick to my comb?

Let's find out!

Round Up These Things

9-inch (23-cm) round balloon

Later You'll Need

balloon from original experiment
plus
paper hole-punch
sheet of tissue paper or other
  thin paper
12-inch (30-cm) long balloon
*NOTE: These experiments work
  best when the humidity is very
  low.*

1 Inflate the balloon to a size that fits easily in your hand.

2 ADULT STEP Tie a knot in the end of the balloon.

3 Rub the inflated balloon back and forth on your hair about 10 times. *NOTE: For best results your hair must be clean, dry, and oil-free.*

4 Slowly pull the balloon away from your hair and hold it close to, but not touching, your head. Your hair will lift and stick to the balloon.

So Now We Know

When you run a comb through your hair, both the comb and your hair become electrically charged. When electric charges are different, they try to stick to each other. The comb and your hair have different charges, so your hair moves toward the comb. This is what happened when you rubbed the balloon against your hair. Your hair stuck to the balloon.

More Fun Things to Know and Do

1 Electric charges can make small pieces of paper fly through the air toward a balloon.

- Use the hole-punch to cut 10 to 15 small circles from the sheet of paper.

- Separate the circles and spread them out on a table.

- Charge the inflated round balloon again by rubbing it on your hair as before.

- Hold the balloon close to, but not touching, the paper circles. Watch what happens to the paper circles.

2 The longer the balloon, the more surface there is that can be charged. If a balloon has a large enough charge, it can stick to a wall.

- Inflate the long balloon and charge it by rubbing it on your hair as before.

- Gently touch the charged side of the balloon against the wall, then let go. Watch what happens to the balloon.

1 Spread the towel across a table. The towel will help prevent the flashlight parts from rolling off the table.

2 ADULT STEP Unscrew the bulb section of the flashlight.

3 ADULT STEP Remove the bulb by snapping out the plastic base that holds the bulb in place.

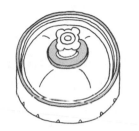

4 Remove the batteries.

5 ADULT STEP Cut a piece of aluminum foil 2 inches (5 cm) wide and as long as needed for the experiment.

6 Fold the foil in half lengthwise three times to make a thin strip ¼ inch (0.63 cm) wide.

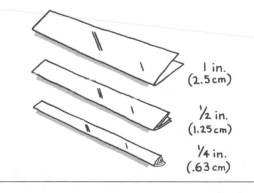

1 in. (2.5 cm)

½ in. (1.25 cm)

¼ in. (.63 cm)

7 Use the foil strip to connect the bulb to one of the batteries so that the bulb glows. *NOTE: Try to do this without looking at the drawing on the following page until after the next step.*

8 Ask a helper to hold the parts as you decide how they should be connected. If you need help, ask your helper to read the following clues one at a time:

- One end of the foil strip touches only one end of the battery.

- The other end of the foil strip wraps around the base of the bulb.

- The metal base of the bulb touches the end of the battery opposite the end the foil touches.

So Now We Know

The bulb in a flashlight lights up when electricity flows through it. The electricity causes the wire in the bulb to get hot and glow.

9 After you discover how to light the bulb, darken the room to see the light better.

More Fun Things to Know and Do

The battery pushes electricity through the foil and bulb. The amount of "push" is doubled by stacking two batteries with the "outty" and "inny" ends together. *NOTE: Stacking more than two batteries will burn out the bulb.*

- Tape the two batteries together so that the "outty" and "inny" ends are together.

- Using the 16-inch (40-cm) foil strip, light the bulb as before.

Appendix A
Red Cabbage Juice Indicator

Purpose

To prepare red cabbage juice to use as an indicator to test for acids and bases in some of the experiments in this book.

Materials

knife (to be handled only by an adult)
cutting board
½ small head of red cabbage
blender
measuring cup
distilled water
large strainer
large bowl
1-quart (1-liter) jar with lid
wide masking tape
marking pen

Procedure

1 ADULT STEP Using the knife and the cutting board, cut the cabbage into small pieces.

2 Place the cabbage pieces in the blender.

3 Use the cup to add enough water to cover the cabbage in the blender.

4 ADULT STEP **Blend the water and cabbage.**

5 **Hold the strainer over the bowl.**

6 ADULT STEP **Pour the contents of the blender into the strainer.**

7 ADULT STEP **Pour the cabbage juice from the bowl to the jar, and discard the solid pieces of cabbage left in the strainer.**

8 **Use the tape and marking pen to label the jar Red Cabbage Indicator.**

Red Cabbage
Indicator

9 **Store the Red Cabbage Indicator in a refrigerator until needed so that it does not spoil.**

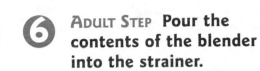

Appendix B
Section Summaries

Air

Air is a mixture of gases, mainly nitrogen and oxygen. The layer of air surrounding the earth is called the **atmosphere**. Air is invisible. Even though it cannot be seen, we know that air exists by the way it affects other things. For example, a cup or a plastic bag may look empty, but each is actually filled with air. The experiment "Spacey" (pages 6–9) demonstrates that air takes up space.

Air also pushes against falling objects. Things fall because of gravity. **Gravity** is a force that pulls everything toward the center of the earth. (Forces are explored in a later section.) Gravity pulls a parachute down, while air pushes against it and slows its fall. The **canopy** is the part of the parachute that catches the air. A canopy can be round like an umbrella or more rectangular like an airplane wing. The experiment "Drifter" (pages 10–13) demonstrates

that air slows falling objects, especially those with a large surface, such as parachutes.

Slow-moving air pushes harder against an object it passes by than fast-moving air does. An airplane or a bird flies when the air under its wings pushes up more than the air above its wings pushes down. A bird flaps its wings to make the air flowing over the top of its wings move faster. The fast-moving air above the wings does not push down as much as the slow-moving air under the wings pushes up. The difference in this pressure above and below the wings results in an upward force called **lift.** Airplane wings are curved so that the air above them moves faster than air below. The experiment "Lifter" (pages 14–17) shows how moving air makes things move.

The gases in air are in constant motion, even though we cannot see or feel them bumping against us. A

bubble is a thin skin of liquid that forms a ball around a gas, such as air. The liquid skin of a soap bubble is made of soap and water. The air inside the bubble pushes outward in all directions on the bubble's skin at the same time that the air outside the skin pushes inward in all directions. This causes the bubble to be shaped like a ball. The experiment "Bubbly" (pages 18–21) encourages children to explore how air and soapy water make bubbles.

Changes

Much of science is the study of changes. Changes are constantly happening all around us. Through the process of **evaporation**, a liquid such as water changes to a gas called **vapor**, due to heat. Even though water vapor is invisible, it is still water. This type of change, in which a material stays the same, is called a **physical change**. Evaporation can be used to separate salt from seawater. In some countries, including the United States, salt is commercially produced by letting the sun evaporate seawater from shallow pools dug near the sea, leaving a deposit of salt crystals. This method of salt production is known as the **solar process**, and the product is called **solar salt**. In the experiment "Dried Out" (pages 24–27), children evaporate the water from saltwater to remove the salt.

Balls bounce because of a physical change called **elasticity** (the ability of a material to return to its original shape after being pushed or pulled out of shape). Elastic materials are said to be **flexible**. The more flexible the material from which a ball is made, the more bounce the ball has. So, the more quickly a ball recovers its shape, the higher it can bounce. In the experiment "Bouncy Blubber" (pages 28–31), children make a soft rubbery material to demonstrate elasticity.

The substance that gives things color is called **pigment**. Black ink is made of a mixture of pigments of several colors. A black ink mark on paper will mix with a drop of water and spread out. As the ink spreads out, the different pigments in the ink separate and the colors can be seen on the paper. The experiment "Mixers" (pages 32–35) lets children separate pigments from various colored inks to make a design.

Another type of change is a chemical change. In a **chemical change**, materials do not stay the same but change into something else. The experiment "Play Clay" (pages 36–39) is a recipe for a chemical change. One clue that a chemical change has occurred in this experiment is that the play clay does not feel or look like the original materials.

Some tests for chemical changes are used to make visible a chemical change that is not readily seen. One such test uses chemicals called **indicators**, which change color in acids and bases. The red cabbage juice made for the experiment "Pucker Up" (pages 40–42) is an indicator. An **acid** is a chemical that tastes sour. (Acids turn red cabbage juice pink to red). The more acidic a food is, the more sour it tastes and the redder it turns red cabbage juice. The acid in lemons and other citric fruit is called citric acid. A **base** is a chemical that tastes bitter and is the opposite of an acid. (Bases turn red cabbage juice blue to green.) The more basic a food is, the more bitter it tastes and

the greener it turns red cabbage juice. A chemical is **neutral** if it is neither acidic nor basic. (Neutral chemicals do not change the color of red cabbage juice, which is purple.) When acids and bases are mixed together, a chemical change called **neutralization** (cancellation) occurs.

Tarnish is a chemical change that causes coins and other metals to lose their bright, shiny appearance and look dull and dark. New, untarnished pennies are a shiny copper color, because one of the metals in pennies is copper. When exposed to air, copper **molecules** (the smallest particles of a material that have all the properties of the material) combine with oxygen molecules in the air, resulting in a chemical change called **oxidation**. Copper oxide is the tarnish on pennies as a result of the oxidation of copper. In the experiment "Shiny Coins" (pages 43–46), tarnish is chemically removed from pennies by soaking them in a vinegar and salt solution.

Magnets

Only some metals are magnetic. Materials that are not magnetic, such as paper and plastics, allow the magnetic field (the area around a magnet in which its magnetic forces can be detected) to pass through the material without any disruptions. This is why a paper can be held between a magnet and a refrigerator door. The experiment "Stickers" (pages 48–51) shows some fun things children can do with magnets to understand the power of magnetic fields.

Near the northernmost point of the earth is a place called the earth's **magnetic north pole**. If a magnet is allowed to swing freely, one pole, or end, will always point toward the earth's magnetic north pole. This end of the magnet is called the **north pole of a magnet**. A **compass** is an instrument used to determine direction by means of a free-swinging magnetic needle. The experiment "North Seekers" (pages 52–55) demonstrates how magnets make a compass work.

The experiment "Pushers" (pages 56–59) shows how magnets react to each other. Magnets move toward each other when the facing poles are different (north to south). When like poles (north and north, or south and south) are held together, the magnets move away from each other.

Forces

A **force** is a push or a pull in a given direction. An **adhesive force** is the pull between different materials, such as the attraction of water to paper. The experiment "Soakers" (pages 62–65) shows how water is **absorbed** (soaked up) by paper towels.

Gravity is the force that pulls everything toward the center of the earth. The experiment "Roly-Poly" (pages 66–69) shows how gravity makes objects roll downhill.

The upward push on an object in a fluid, such as water, is called **buoyancy**. Objects in water sink when their weight is greater than the buoyancy exerted on them by the water. Another factor that determines whether objects sink or float is their density. **Density** is a comparison of **weight** (a force caused by gravity) and size. If two objects weigh the same but are different sizes, the larger object is less dense and more likely to float than the other object is. Buoyancy increases with the weight of the water. Seawater weighs more than freshwater because of the salt in it, so objects float better in the ocean than in freshwater. In the experiment "Floater" (pages 70–73), children

explore buoyancy by molding clay into two different shapes, a ball that sinks and a boat that floats. The difference in the shape of the clay changes its size, and, thus, affects its buoyancy.

Pressure is the amount of force on a certain area. One way that pressure can be reduced is by applying a force over a larger area. The dome shape of an eggshell provides a structure imitated by architects because of its strength. The pressure of a hen's weight on the eggshell is spread down along the curved surface of the egg. Thus, the force is applied over a large area and the egg does not break. In the experiment "Breakable?" (pages 74–77), children see just how hard it can be to break an egg.

Things that are moving will continue to move unless some force stops them. This resistance to change in motion is called **inertia**. Without a seat belt, a person in a car continues to move forward when the car suddenly stops. The seat belt pushes against the person and forces the person to stop with the car. In the experiment "Buckle Up" (pages 78–81), children use models to see what happens when a car suddenly stops and the person in the car isn't wearing a seat belt.

Light

A **shadow** is the dark area cast upon a surface by an object that blocks light. When light cannot pass through a material, a shadow is cast. The length of the shadow depends on where the light is. Shadows made by the sun get shorter as the sun rises higher in the sky. When the sun is directly overhead, little or no shadow is produced. The experiment "Changing" (pages 84–87) shows how shadows change size depending on the position of the light that makes them.

A **rainbow** is an arc-shaped band of colors in the sky. To see a rainbow, there must be water drops in the air and the sun must be behind the viewer. If the sun is higher than 42 degrees above the horizon, no rainbow will appear. Rainbows are produced when white light passes through water in the air and separates into colors. The experiment "Rainbows" (pages 88–91) lets children use water to make rainbows in air and on paper.

Sound

Sounds are made when things **vibrate** (shake or move back and forth repeatedly). The rate at which an object vibrates affects the **pitch** (high or low quality) of the sound produced. As the vibration rate decreases, the pitch gets lower. In the experiment "Musical Glasses" (pages 92–95), children produce musical sounds by tapping on glasses filled with water. Tapping on glass causes the glass and its contents to vibrate. The more water in the glass, the slower the glass vibrates and the lower the pitch. Vibrating glass pushes on the air surrounding it. As the glass molecules move outward, the air is **compressed** (squeezed together). As the molecules move back inward, the compressed air surrounding the glass **expands** (spreads out). Vibrations cause the air to be compressed and expanded repeatedly. These compressions and expansions of the air as sound moves through it are called **sound waves**. Sound travels in waves as it moves through any substance.

A telephone works not because the telephone wires vibrate, but because the vibrations of voice sounds are changed into electric signals. The signals travel along wires from the mouthpiece of one telephone to the earpiece of another telephone, where the signals are changed back into sound. In the experiment "String Telephone" (pages 96–99), children make telephones that use cups as both the mouthpiece and the earpiece. The vibrations of the speaker's voice make one cup vibrate. These vibrations travel along the string to the other cup, which vibrates and the speaker's voice is heard.

When a person chews, the teeth hit against each other and against the food in the person's mouth. This causes the teeth to vibrate. The bones in the head pass these vibrations along to the ears. The experiment "Musical Teeth" (pages 100–103) demonstrates that sound waves traveling through solids are louder than sound waves traveling through air.

Electricity

All **matter** (anything that takes up space and has weight) is made up of **atoms** (tiny particles from which all things are made). Atoms are made of positive electric charges called **protons** and negative electric charges called **electrons**. There are an equal number of protons and electrons in each atom. A comb pulled through hair will rub some of the electrons off the hair, leaving the hair with more protons than electrons. The hair is then positively charged, and the comb is negatively charged. The different charges on the comb and the hair cause the comb and the hair to be attracted to each other. This buildup of stationary electric charges in one place is called **static electricity**. In the experiment "Attractive" (pages 106–109), children use static electricity to make a balloon stick to their hair, paper, and a wall.

A **battery** is a device that uses chemicals to produce **current electricity** (a form of energy associated with the movement of electric charges). A flashlight bulb glows when electricity flows through an **electric circuit** (the path that electricity follows), which includes the battery, a foil strip, and a fine wire filament inside the flashlight bulb. When the electricity reaches the wire filament, the wire becomes hot and glows. In the experiment "Flashlight" (pages 110–113), children take apart a flashlight to see how it works.

Glossary

absorb To soak up.

acid A chemical that tastes sour and turns red cabbage juice pink to red.

adhesive force The pull or attraction between different materials, such as that between water and paper.

air A mixture of gases, mainly nitrogen and oxygen.

atmosphere The layer of air surrounding the earth.

atoms Tiny particles from which all things are made.

base A chemical that tastes bitter, is the opposite of an acid, and turns red cabbage juice blue to green.

battery A device that uses chemicals to produce an electric current.

bubble A thin skin of liquid that forms a ball around a gas such as air.

buoyancy The upward push on an object placed in a fluid, such as water or air.

canopy The part of a parachute that catches the air.

chemical change A change, such as oxidation, in which materials change into something else.

compass An instrument used to determine direction by means of a free-swinging magnetic needle that points to the earth's magnetic north pole.

compress To squeeze together.

current electricity A form of energy associated with the movement of electric charges.

density A comparison of weight and size.

elasticity The ability of a material to return to its original shape after being pushed or pulled out of shape.

electric circuit The path that electricity follows.

electrons Negative electric charges in an atom.

evaporation The process by which a liquid changes to a gas due to heat.

expand To spread out.

flexible Having elasticity.

force A push or pull in a given direction.

gravity The force that pulls everything toward the center of the earth.

hypothesis An educated guess about the solution to a problem.

indicators Chemicals that change color in acids and bases.

inertia The resistance to change in motion.

lift An upward force.

magnetic field The area around a magnet in which its magnetic forces can be detected.

magnetic north pole The area near the northernmost point on the earth toward which the north poles of all magnets are attracted.

matter Anything that takes up space and has weight.

molecule The smallest particle of a material that has all the properties of the material.

neutral Being a chemical that is neither an acid nor a base.

neutralization A chemical change that cancels acids and bases by combining them.

north pole of a magnet The end of a magnet that points to the earth's magnetic north pole.

oxidation A chemical change in which oxygen in the air combines with a substance.

physical change A change, such as evaporation, that does not produce a new substance.

pigment A substance that gives color to things.

pitch The high or low quality of a sound.

pressure The amount of force on a certain area.

protons Positive electric charges in an atom.

rainbow An arc-shaped band of colors in the sky.

shadow The dark area cast upon a surface by an object that blocks light.

solar process The production of salt by the evaporation of seawater.

solar salt Salt produced by the solar process.

sound waves Compression and expansion of a material as vibrations move through it.

static electricity The buildup of stationary electric charges in one place.

tarnish A chemical change that causes metals to become dull and dark due to oxidation.

vapor The gas state of a liquid.

vibrate To shake or move back and forth repeatedly.

weight A force caused by gravity.

Index